one step at a time

Supporting children's
progress towards
the stepping stones

contents

Introduction and Aims

The Foundation Stage Guidance document is a very welcome tool for Early Years practitioners. It is felt that it could be useful to have some idea of the stages prior to the "Stepping Stones" when planning for some children.

It is intended that this document is used as an aid to planning and assessment alongside any specific provision/support required for children who have special educational needs or disabilities.

The format of the document is not designed to be a hierarchical checklist or age-related. It is recognised that children develop at different rates and, in some cases, idiosyncratically.

The very early stages of the document are generic across all areas of learning.

Principles of Good Practice

As with all children, abilities may progress at different rates across the areas of the Foundation Stage and this may vary significantly in children who have special educational needs.

Collaborative working practices and liaison with parents and other professionals are vital.

Good home/school links need to be established in whatever learning environment the child is.

Practitioners need to:

- Take time to observe and listen
- React and feedback to children
- Model signs and language
- Provide opportunities for additional language support including mother tongue and their personal language
- Provide consistent opportunities and routines
- Allow time for children to respond
- Understand that some learning may be idiosyncratic
- Understand that activities need pacing
- Understand child's own learning style
- Adapt environment as necessary
- Ensure children have concrete experiences
- Use object cues and symbols
- Adapt recording methods if necessary

towards the stepping stones

Early Developmental Steps

STEPPING STONES	EXAMPLES OF WHAT CHILDREN DO
Show reflex responses to hearing, vision, smell, touch and taste	• Move eyes when light is shone • Move body in response to sound • Tolerate being stroked on hand • Accept liquidised food spread on lips • Respond to familiar aromas • Look towards a visual cue • Turn towards sounds • Positively react to touch • Explore taste with tongue or mouth • Begin to show different responses to different smells
Show reactive responses to familiar people, objects and situations	• Consistently react to familiar adults, children and pets • Begin to show awareness of everyday routines • Respond consistently to familiar objects
Actively explore people, objects and tactile materials	• Through own body movements shows interest by preferred method of touch, for example: reaching, grasping, holding
Respond to familiar sounds, cues or gestures to express basic needs, wants and feelings in response to their immediate environment	• Show an understanding through their own communication method, for example: eye pointing, turning away • Show excitement by body movements/vocalisations to everyday routines, for example: bath time, snack and drink time

towards the stepping stones

Early Developmental Steps

STEPPING STONES	EXAMPLES OF WHAT CHILDREN DO
Children make gestures or sounds to express simple needs, wants or feelings in response to their immediate environment	• Look towards object/person that gives a clue as to what they want • Reach or point to desired object • Use facial expression to communicate feelings • Use initial sounds or approximations of words, for example "ccc" for car
Show anticipation in response to familiar people, routines, activities or actions	• Facial expression changes when told, for example: "drink-time", or "swimming" • Body movements • Show excitement prior to familiar activity
Show anticipation in response to familiar people, routines, activities, actions and respond appropriately	• Looking towards school bag when told it is school time, reaching for cup at drink-time
Able to communicate simple likes and dislikes Begin to make simple choices by a preferred method	• Smiling and looking for more • Using switch to answer "yes" or "no" • Positive or negative vocalisations in response to sensory experience • Choosing by eye pointing with real objects
Manipulate objects, toys or other equipment Begin to use trial and error techniques	• Repeating an action to gain desired effect • Turning, pulling, pressing activity toys • Placing and manipulating inset puzzle pieces

Personal, Social and Emotional Development

SENSE OF COMMUNITY	
STEPPING STONES	**EXAMPLES OF WHAT CHILDREN DO**
Copy adult's use of voice to express emotions	• Laugh, show sadness, show fright when adult shows these emotions
Copy when adult uses puppets or toys to express emotions	• Pretend to sob when teddy is sad
Show emotions linked to pictures/symbols	• Laugh at picture of smile • Smile when given thumbs up sign • Show sad and happy expressions when requested by adult
Express emotions	• Able to tell adult what makes them happy or sad by preferred means of communication, for example: points to picture of birthday cake to indicate what makes them happy

towards the stepping stones

Personal, Social and Emotional Development

FORM RELATIONSHIPS

STEPPING STONES	EXAMPLES OF WHAT CHILDREN DO
Become aware of others	• Show interest in what peers are doing in group activity • Show awareness of what others are doing in the room
Contribute appropriately in one to one situations in taking turns	• Able to wait for turn for a biscuit without grabbing or making a fuss
Contribute appropriately with support in groups of up to three	• Able to play simple lotto game with adult support with another child

SELF-CARE

STEPPING STONES	EXAMPLES OF WHAT CHILDREN DO
Able to choose from a selection of two objects	• Choose from two fruits at snack time • Choose what colour apron to have on
Understand how resources are used	• Choose own activity from limited choice and use appropriately, for example: play with cars on mat, make marks on paper with felt tip, attempt to cut paper with scissors

towards the stepping stones

Personal, Social and Emotional Development

DISPOSITIONS AND ATTITUDES

STEPPING STONES	EXAMPLES OF WHAT CHILDREN DO
Show increasing concentration Show increasing engagement	• Play with toy selected by adult for increasing amount of time, for example: from 1 minute to 10 minutes • Follow toy when it is taken away • Play with toy selected independently
Able to concentrate with decreasing support	• Sit with adult in small group throughout activity • Allow adult to withdraw after activity has started • Stay on task at activity with limited verbal support
Show increasing willingness to explore materials	• Put hands in tray containing different materials such as beads, lentils, sand and foam • Move hands around in tray • Remove hands then puts them back in tray
Shows increasing engagement with activities	• Watch other children engaged in finger painting • Willing to put fingers in paint after others have had a go • Willing to put on apron and put hands in paint

towards the stepping stones

Communication, Language and Literacy

LANGUAGE FOR COMMUNICATION AND THINKING

STEPPING STONES	EXAMPLES OF WHAT CHILDREN DO
Imitate adults using simple body movements linking to single words	• Wave for goodbye • Thumbs up for well done
Communicate likes and dislikes for a range of sensory experiences through consistent vocalisations/gestures	• Grimace or withdraw when hands put on playdough • Smile when smelling roses • Make happy sound when listening to favourite song
Initiate songs/rhymes by vocalisation or gesture	• Make a familiar action associated with a particular song, for example: signs bus for "The Wheels on the Bus"
Copy sound and rhythm in familiar songs	• Hum to a recognisable tune • Sing song using own jargon • Reproduce sounds and rhythm at other times
Produce first approximation of real words	• Say "ink" for drink, "ju" for juice • Bbb for bus
Use single words	• Cup, drink • Use words appropriately, such as "more" for more drink, "up" for carry
Use two word phrases/gestures/signs to convey meaning	• Say "my car" when another child tries to take toy away

towards the stepping stones

Communication, Language and Literacy

LANGUAGE FOR COMMUNICATION AND THINKING

STEPPING STONES	EXAMPLES OF WHAT CHILDREN DO
Co-ordinate body movements and words	• Lift up arms and utter "up"
Use non-verbal communication to support single/two word utterances	• Eye point to cup for drink
Engage in language games	• Put out hand for "Round and Round the Garden"
Can respond to simple instruction	• Sit down when asked
Combine three words, signs or symbols to communicate meaning	• Able to communicate "Carly shoe wet"
Use negatives in 2 word phrases	• "no juice" when offered.
Use facial expression and intonation to enhance meaning	• Rub upper arm whilst saying "cold"
Follow two component instructions	• Able to select a certain toy and give it to another child upon request from adult, or other child
Show an understanding of simple positional language	• Put the doll in the pram when asked • Place the puzzle on the table when asked

towards the stepping stones

Communication, Language and Literacy

READING

STEPPING STONES	EXAMPLES OF WHAT CHILDREN DO
Choose stories/songs using symbols	• Point to symbol 'spider' for "Incy Wincy Spider"
Choose stories/songs using objects of reference	• Indicate teddy bear for 3 bears story
Match stories/songs from a selection of 3 symbols	• Match picture of bear to "Goldilocks "story
Join in with key word/repetitive phrase in story with adult support	• With encouragement shake head for "no" in "How Do I Put It On?"
Joins in with key word/repetitive phrase spontaneously	• Joins in "nah" in "Bartholemew Bear " • Says "Eat up Gemma"
Look at a book with adult	• Able to concentrate on short picture book with adult for short period of time
Show spontaneous interest in books	• Choose a book and look at pictures independently

WORD RECOGNITION

STEPPING STONES	EXAMPLES OF WHAT CHILDREN DO
Match object to object	• Find matching objects, such as toy cars
Match objects to symbols	• Match biscuit symbol with snack time
Recognise symbols of everyday object	• React appropriately when shown symbol for bus, for example: point to coat
Recognise pictures in books	• Use gestures or symbols when looking at pictures in book, such as dog when reading Spot
Fill in missing word in familiar story or rhyme	• Indicates last word in phrase using speech or symbol, such as "He was too...big," in "Dear Zoo"

Communication, Language and Literacy

HANDWRITING

STEPPING STONES	EXAMPLES OF WHAT CHILDREN DO
Show awareness of cause and effect relating to manual dexterity	• Look towards hand when engaged in tactile activities, such as making impressions in sand
Show pride in results of tactile activities	• Indicate pleasure in making cuts in play dough
Attempt to make marks with increasing confidence and control	• Hold marker in preferred grip and makes marks on paper • Put fingers in paint and makes marks on paper
Form vertical and horizontal lines with physical prompts	• Adult holds child hand to track a horizontal line
Form vertical and horizontal lines independently	• Make mark actions without adult support
Explore a range of mark making tools	• Choose from a choice of thin or thick felt tip pens

TOWARDS SYMBOLIC REPRESENTATION

STEPPING STONES	EXAMPLES OF WHAT CHILDREN DO
Join in with repetitive phrase spontaneously	• Blow during "I'll huff and I'll puff" in 3 Little Pigs
Explore every day items and begin to act out simple routines	• Pretend tissue is a cloth to wipe table
Use real objects appropriately	• Pretend to drink from empty cup
Explore less familiar objects and begin to act out simple actions	• Pretend to feed teddy with cup

Mathematical Development

NUMBERS AS LABELS FOR COUNTING

STEPPING STONES	EXAMPLES OF WHAT CHILDREN DO
Show awareness of number songs and rhymes	• Listen to number songs containing numbers up to five • Use objects of reference to choose a familiar number song • Use symbols to choose a familiar number song • Vocalise or demonstrate non-verbal reaction, for example: eye movement when choosing a familiar number/song
Respond to numbers said/sung in order	• Vocalise or demonstrate non-verbal reaction as numbers are said or sung backwards from ten • Use fingers to show an understanding of the numbers
Show of awareness of counting	• Show a reaction when objects or children are counted, for example: the adult counts 1,2,3 when putting bricks in box
Show a willingness to explore quantity	• Manipulate small objects when exploring their uses, for example: building towers, joining bricks, threading cotton reels and lining up cars

towards the stepping stones

Mathematical Development

SHAPE SPACE AND MEASURES

STEPPING STONES	EXAMPLES OF WHAT CHILDREN DO
Show a willingness to explore 2D or 3D shapes	• Explore large and small everyday objects, for example: balls, saucers, bricks
Demonstrate awareness of position with everyday objects	• Make a tower of nesting beakers with the largest at the bottom • Indicate by vocalisation, signing, gesture or touching where objects are, for example: the cup is on the tray
Be able to follow simple verbal or non verbal instructions on position or direction	• Play with wheeled toys and push them forward and backwards on request • Go down the slide on request, (words or gesture)

USE MATHEMATICAL IDEAS

STEPPING STONES	EXAMPLES OF WHAT CHILDREN DO
Show an awareness that sets can be broken down	• Make a choice from 2 objects, for example: biscuits at snack time

towards the stepping stones

Knowledge and Understanding of the World

DESIGNING AND MAKING SKILLS

STEPPING STONES	EXAMPLES OF WHAT CHILDREN DO
Show interest in construction materials	• Willing to explore a variety of materials, for example: stickle bricks, lego, blocks
Begin to build with limited materials	• Build with large sponge bricks, which require simple positioning next to/on top of each other
Able to make a choice	• Choose construction toys from a choice of two shown either verbally or by pointing or eye movement
Is willing to manipulate materials	• Explore pliable materials using both hands • Explore textures comparing and contrasting feel… expressing a preference • Require help from adult when exploring new construction materials
Understand that tools can enhance manipulative techniques	• Use simple tools independently such as rolling pin
Use a range of materials in collage making	• Choose from a limited range of textured material, for example: to make a tree trunk
Know what tools are needed for a task	• Indicate using preferred methods that a glue spreader is needed to spread glue
Know what materials they will need to complete a task	• Choose circles of card to make wheels on a car
Use construction materials to build objects	• Put foam blocks together to make tower
Attach together 3D shapes to make simple representational models	• Make a car using two blocks of duplo lego
Be able to plan	• Select from symbols what they would like to make

Knowledge and Understanding of the World

EXPLORATION AND INVESTIGATION-MATCHING AND SORTING

STEPPING STONES	EXAMPLES OF WHAT CHILDREN DO
Match objects from a choice of two	• Match object when shown by adult, then independently • Match individual objects felt in a feely bag • Match objects in home corner
Match attribute to object	• Match smell to real object such as oranges and bananas
Match two symbols of objects	• Willing to take part in simple lotto game
Match sounds heard to real objects	• Recognise that buzzer goes with alarm clock

towards the stepping stones

Knowledge and Understanding of the World

ICT

STEPPING STONES	EXAMPLES OF WHAT CHILDREN DO
Begin to show an interest in technological equipment	• Show reaction to stimulus, for example: television, projectors, tape recorder
Understand that they can have an effect on technological equipment	• Use one then two switches to operate computer/switch toys showing an understanding of cause and effect • Point to requested household objects • Use a 'Big Mac' to respond to questions/join in story

EXPLORATION AND INVESTIGATION

STEPPING STONES	EXAMPLES OF WHAT CHILDREN DO
Show an awareness of his/her environment	• Track consistently a preferred visual stimulus • Manipulate objects to produce sounds
Show an awareness of differences of texture	• Show preference by their own preferred method towards a chosen texture from a choice of two • Manipulate two objects together to compare textures or size
Show awareness of object permanence	• Look for objects when they fall off tray/are taken away from them through voice or gesture 'Where has it gone?' • Explore simple toys acting out associated actions, for example: pushing a car and making a noise
Show awareness of people and objects in the pre-school/school environment	• Ask where staff member or peer has gone upon leaving the room
Begin to ask questions of adults by preferred method of communication	• Indicate that they want an answer, for example: point to a person and make interrogative sound

Knowledge and Understanding of the World

SENSE OF TIME

STEPPING STONES	EXAMPLES OF WHAT CHILDREN DO
Begin to show awareness of self and family	• Show increased response to mother/father/carer • Recognise photos/videos of family members
Relate pictures to people	• Show preference for classroom staff • Recognise staff members in class groups • Name members when shown photos

SENSE OF PLACE

STEPPING STONES	EXAMPLES OF WHAT CHILDREN DO
Show awareness of home	• Show response to and expectation of different settings, for example: bathroom and bedroom
Show an awareness of nursery/school environment	• Recognise journey that will take him/her to nursery • Recognise areas of the nursery
Relate symbols and pictures to the real world	• Point to symbols for example of tree, house, car

CULTURES AND BELIEFS

STEPPING STONES	EXAMPLES OF WHAT CHILDREN DO
Begin to show awareness of special events	• Respond to special events such as birthdays, celebrations by smiling
Show a positive reaction to own culture	• Show enjoyment of family celebrations, food, and religious events (if appropriate), language

Physical Development

MOVEMENT, SENSE OF SPACE

STEPPING STONES	EXAMPLES OF WHAT CHILDREN DO
Reach for an activity offered	• Move hands or arms in response to familiar toy being offered in close proximity
Start to move towards object within familiar environment	• Respond and move towards toy placed at certain distance, using preferred method, for example: turning, rolling, shuffling
Experience free fall sensation	• Happy to be joggled on adult's knee • Happy to make small jump when assisted by adult
Begin to move around the room	• Roll, shuffle on request to certain familiar adult • Move towards toy of their choice
Move round the room on request	• Return to chair on request • Move back to chair or carpet in daily routine, for example: at circle time, go back to chair

USING EQUIPMENT, TOOLS AND MATERIALS

STEPPING STONES	EXAMPLES OF WHAT CHILDREN DO
Begin to explore large equipment	• Move freely in soft play area • Use small slide with adult support • Attempt to climb up small steps • Begin to use wheeled toys with adult support, for example: will sit on a trike if held by adult
Begin to explore small equipment	• Handle toys or other equipment, beginning to use trial and error techniques • Handle bean bags, balls of different sizes and textures, quoits • Explore the properties of equipment, for example: rolling and sliding • Use different actions for small equipment, for example: throwing, pushing • Attempt to hit or kick a ball on request
Handle tools, objects, construction and malleable materials safely and with increasing control	• Engage in activities requiring hand and eye co-ordination such as stirring, pouring, rolling, cutting

Physical Development

HEALTH AND BODILY AWARENESS

STEPPING STONES	EXAMPLES OF WHAT CHILDREN DO
Begins to cooperate with simple hygiene routines	• Put hands into water and move fingers, tolerate adults washing and drying hands • Tolerate a toothbrush in the mouth • Tolerate adult brushing their teeth, put toothbrush into mouth and suck toothpaste from brush
Develop a list of likes and dislikes, connected to food	• Experimentation with different tastes and textures • Able to point to symbols of food on request
Begin to show an awareness of when they are hot or cold	• After exercise to feel their skin when encouraged by adult • Able to show when they are hot or cold using preferred method of communication, reinforced by signs and or symbols
Show awareness of body parts	• Point to parts of body when responding to picture cue • Point to parts of body on response to verbal and/or signed cue

towards the stepping stones

Creative Development

MEDIA AND MATERIALS

STEPPING STONES	EXAMPLES OF WHAT CHILDREN DO
Begin to explore paint	• Tolerate paint/sensory stimuli on hands/body parts • Finger paint independently
Use tools to apply paint	• Begin to manipulate tools, for example brushes, rollers, sponges • Use sponges/objects to print simple 2 D shapes
Use colours appropriately	• Choose colour by preferred method to use in stated task, for example: what colour do you want to paint the car?
Use increasing range of colours	• Blend 2 colours together using hands/brush • Free paint using a range of 3 colours • Free paint using a range of 5 colours
Free paint recognising boundaries of field	• Paint on paper not table using a range of tools, or hands
Use appropriate tools for medium	• Choose glue spreader to spread paste on paper • Choose fine brush for water colour
Use a range of materials in collage making Indicate materials needed to complete a task	• Select from a range of textured material for tree trunk • Select appropriate collage materials

towards the stepping stones

Creative Development

MUSIC	
STEPPING STONES	**EXAMPLES OF WHAT CHILDREN DO**
Recognise familiar tunes/songs	• Respond to familiar songs by vocalisation, gesture facial expression • Copy sounds made in familiar songs • Fill in missing words from familiar rhymes, poems, songs by using sounds or gestures
Explore a range of musical instruments including the voice	• Make random sounds independently on a range of instruments • Make an approximation towards clapping and banging to music • Make an approximation of familiar songs /tunes in spontaneous play • Shake instrument in time with songs/music
Recognise musical instruments Play instruments by plucking, banging, shaking, blowing	• Match instrument to instrument, instrument to picture • Imitate adult
Accompany familiar songs in a range of ways	• Start and stop clapping independently during a song • Copy simple clapping patterns with visual prompts
Take part as a member of a group	• Play instruments along with music/others
Match sound heard to symbol of object	• In circle time when sound is heard on tape will choose correct object from two • Choose correct object from wider choice

Creative Development

IMAGINATION	
STEPPING STONES	**EXAMPLES OF WHAT CHILDREN DO**
Imitate adult's movements in playing with props	• Make puppet jump or sleep
Imitate adult's movements/actions when pretending Spontaneously show imaginative responses	• Pretend to be monster, animals • Act independently in spontaneous play, for example growl when playing with a teddy
Copy adult's behaviour with toys	• Rock a baby • Give teddy a "drink"
Copy adult's use of voice to express emotions	• Pretend to laugh, cry, be cross
Copy physical movements	• Shake hands, stamp feet
Contribute appropriately to one to one and small group role-play	• Pretend to feed baby when encouraged by adult
Play with small toys in a simple symbolic manner	• "Drink" from toy tea cup making slurping sound

towards the stepping stones

acknowledgments

Text by the Redbridge Early Years Development & Childcare Partnership

Thanks to
Maggie Baldwin · Hyleford School · Clare Warner · Joyce Westwood ·
Ethel Davis School · Sue Bayliss · Madeleine Swindle · Anne Davies ·
Woodford Family Centre · Jennifer Smith · Thackery Drive Family Centre ·
Early Years Assessment Service and Centre · Chris Chappell ·
Redbridge Pre-school Home Visiting Service · Marlene Cross · Carol Frost ·
Jenni Braysher · Yvonne Shatter · Hatton School · Redbridge EYDCP ·

photographs

Ethel Davis School · Redbridge Pre-school Home Visiting Service ·
Hyleford School and Loxford Crèche · Oakfield Pre-school Playgroup ·
Woodford Family Centre ·

Designed by Clinch Graphic Communication
Printed in England by Neartone Ltd, Nottingham